The Shaker Book of the Garden

With a FACSIMILE of the *ORIGINAL* *Gardener's Manual* of 1843

WORDS & PICTURES BY
LORRAINE HARRISON

BARRON'S

First edition for the United States, its territories
and dependencies, and Canada published in 2004 by
BARRON'S EDUCATIONAL SERIES, INC.

This book was conceived,
designed, and produced by
THE IVY PRESS LIMITED
The Old Candlemakers
West Street, Lewes
East Sussex BN7 2NZ, U.K.

Creative Director *Peter Bridgewater*
Publisher *Sophie Collins*
Editorial Director *Steve Luck*
Senior Project Editor *Caroline Earle*
Design Manager *Tony Seddon*
Illustrations *Lorraine Harrison*

All inquiries should be addressed to:
Barron's Educational Series, Inc.
250 Wireless Blvd.
Hauppauge, NY 11788
www.barronseduc.com

International Standard Book No.:
0-7641-5711-6
Library of Congress Catalog No.: 2003106929

Printed and bound in China
9 8 7 6 5 4 3 2 1

Contents

Heaven on Earth

INTRODUCTION

"If you would have a lovely garden, you should live a LOVELY LIFE.*"*

SHAKER SAYING

THE SHAKERS, or United Society of Believers in the First and Second Appearance of Christ, is the best known of the many communities of religious dissenters that flourished in America during the eighteenth and nineteenth centuries. Originally known as the "Shaking Quakers," due to the violent trembling and shaking they experienced during worship, the sect began in mid-eighteenth century Manchester, England.

It was there that a charismatic factory girl, Ann Lee (1736–84), later known to her followers as Mother Ann, was imprisoned several times for her beliefs. During her last incarceration, she had a vision that revealed to her that carnality was at the root of the world's evils. She dreamed of founding a Utopian society, a "heaven on earth," in the New World, where men and women could live equal, though celibate, lives. Upon her release from prison in 1774 she, along with eight followers, set sail for America to make her vision reality.

SHAKER SETTLEMENTS WERE MODELS OF "HEAVEN ON EARTH."

From such small beginnings and after many difficult struggles, the first Shaker settlement was founded near Albany, New York, during the latter years of the eighteenth century. Over time, other Shaker settlements were established in Connecticut, Indiana, Kentucky, Massachusetts, Maine, New Hampshire, and Ohio. Mother Ann's dream that followers would "flock like doves to the windows" was finally realized—in 1847 the Shakers numbered approximately 6,000. Eventually, these communities chose to live separate from the rest of society, away from those whom they regarded as inhabiting "the World." These close Shaker settlements were founded on a shared belief system, which included a commitment to common property, the confession of one's sins, sexual equality, pacifism, and celibacy.

The strict celibacy law obviously meant that no children were born into the Shaker faith. New members of the Shaker communities could join only after a period of reflection and contemplation; "miraculous conversions" were frowned upon. All members had to be older than 21 years of age, free from debt or other obligations, be happy to give their possessions to the community, and accept wholeheartedly the Society's rules and authority. If they were already married, the permission of their spouse would have to be sought.

Sadly, from the latter part of the nineteenth century, Shaker numbers began to decline and the first communities closed. Increasing industrialization, a dwindling of religious fervor, along with the apparent rigidity of some of the more stringent rules and laws imposed by the communities, all contributed to the diminishing appeal of the Shaker way of life. Today one community remains, at Sabbathday Lake, Maine, with only a small number of Believers.

The Shakers applied their exacting standards of simplicity, purity, and perfection to all their activities, following Mother Ann's entreaty, "whatever is fashioned, let it be plain and simple and for the good." Their buildings, along with their products, such as furniture, textiles, and tools, were noted for their functionality, high quality, and attention to detail, as well as for their beauty. Likewise, their horticultural seeds were "pure and genuine." However, it is not only the Shakers' approach to their industrious herb and seed production businesses that is of interest to the modern-day gardener, but also their careful and vigilant tending of the earth, which has much to teach us.

The Gardener's Manual

THYME

The Shakers lived in very close communities with their fellow believers, but they interacted commercially with those in what they termed "the World" with great success. They operated with particular business acumen in the areas of herb and seed production.

The Shakers were the first producers of commercial seed in America. Their seed varieties were not only "carefully selected" to be "those that are most useful," but their quality was unsurpassable. They marketed their goods with flair, becoming the first seed growers to offer their seeds for sale to the kitchen gardener in small paper envelopes, the forerunners of our commercial seed packets today. Farmers were sold bulk quantities of seed in large cloth bags.

In 1835 the United Society published *The Gardener's Manual,* written by Charles F. Crosman. It sold 16,000 copies and a revised version by Franklin Barber appeared in 1843. The *Manual* was sold through their seed distributors to those customers seeking "plain and practical direction" on vegetable production, for "a garden is very necessary and useful, almost every body admits." With such high-quality seed and sound advice, few gardeners could fail to grow healthy and nutritious fruit and vegetables.

The Shaker community at New Lebanon in Columbia County made a staggering $10,000 from seed sales in 1853. The growing and processing of medicinal herbs was also an area in which these communities excelled; there was even a demand from as far away as Europe for their healing preparations, which had a reputation for great purity. At their peak, the combined Shaker settlements worked something in the order of 200 acres of physic gardens.

Yet the real appeal of the Shaker gardening tradition for the modern-day gardener lies not in their undoubted commercial success,

APPLES: EDEN'S FRUIT

but in their spiritual and holistic approach to tending the earth. While *The Gardener's Manual* offers much sound practical advice for the kitchen gardener, it also provides sustainable guidelines for producing a productive, beautiful, and harmonious gardening environment, a veritable "heaven on earth." If closely observed, the well-tended garden can provide an instructive example of how to live life respecting, nurturing, and harvesting God's bounty.

Order, Usefulness, and Beauty

THE SHAKER GARDEN

"The GARDEN *is said to be the index of the owner's mind. If this be true, many who otherwise might be acquitted, must be judged to possess minds susceptible of much improvement in* ORDER, USEFULNESS, *and* BEAUTY."

THE GARDENER'S MANUAL, 1843

IT IS PROBABLY an exceptional modern-day gardener who would wish his or her garden to be seen by others as the index of their minds. Most of us feel a distinct lack of "order, usefulness, and beauty" not only in our gardens, but often in our minds and lives.

Yet, if we begin to apply the simple Shaker philosophy of performing each task to the best of our abilities in our kitchen gardens; if we nurture our soil, diligently tend our plants, and respect the fellow creatures who inhabit our plots, then the result is likely to be not only a productive garden, but one of organic, sustainable beauty. It's a model we might usefully apply to the rest of our lives.

ORDER MADE BEAUTIFUL IN THE SHAKER GARDEN.

Simplicity and appropriateness are the keys to creating a sympathetic Shaker-style garden. Forget elaborate plans and vain ambitions. As a writer in the magazine *The Shaker* commented back in 1871, "the fewer wants, the more happiness." *The Gardener's Manual* gave sound advice on the first principles that should be observed when beginning a kitchen garden. Although some of this advice will apply today only to those with the most commodious of sites, all gardeners will find something of use, however modest their plot.

POSITION YOUR GARDEN FOR MAXIMUM SUNSHINE.

Site

Wherever possible, choose sunny, even land that slopes gently to the south or east. For convenience, a kitchen garden should be close to the house and, for protection from winds, enclosed by a high wall or fence.

Soil

Every gardener covets the "deep, dry, light, and rich" soil described in *The Gardener's Manual.* Do not worry if your soil is not naturally so because it shall "be made so by art." Drain if too wet; plow if too shallow; manure if too poor; and if your land is too stony, fill wheelbarrows full with the offenders and remove from the site: "Thus should every impediment and obstruction to a good sweet soil, be reversed or removed, by industry and art."

STRAWBERRIES NEED A LARGE AREA TO GROW WELL.

Size

A quarter of an acre will provide a family of six with most of the vegetables they can raise from seed. If fruit trees and space-consuming crops, such as strawberries and early potatoes are desired, a bigger plot would be advisable.

Shape

Square or rectangular plots are both convenient and orderly in appearance. The Shakers obviously felt strongly about the latter point because one of their Millennial Laws (a set of rules published between 1821 and 1860, which aimed to standardize the behavior of Believers) prescribes the following concerning the layout of gardens: "all walks must be laid straight, fields laid out square, and fences built straight."

A WELL-ORDERED AND ORGANIZED PLOT

Tools and implements

Few gardeners today have plows and harrows, but a rake, hoe, spade, trowel, watering pot or can, pruning knife, shears, twine, bean poles, and stakes are as indispensable to the modern gardener as they were to the Shakers 150 years ago.

Put Your Hands to Work and Your Hearts to God

GARDEN TOOLS

"Go work with ardent COURAGE,
And SOW *with willing hand*
The seed o'er barren deserts
And o'er the FERTILE LAND."

MOTHER ANN LEE

THE SHAKERS are perhaps best known today for their furniture, which is both beautifully made and classically simple in design. To the modern eye, it seems the very embodiment of the Shaker philosophy of "order, usefulness, and beauty." Just as the English Arts and Crafts writer and designer William Morris (1834–96) was later to proclaim—"Have nothing in your houses that you do not know to be useful, or believe to be beautiful"—the Shakers believed that "beauty rests in utility." Whether constructing a building, a chair, or a garden tool, the same level

A FRUIT OF FAITHFUL LABOR

of attention to detail was applied, reflecting their religious ideal of doing every task, no matter how humble, to the best of one's ability.

Mother Ann's teachings urged: "Equality in labour, all working for each and each for all." However, the Shakers did not believe that labor should be harder than it need be. They were innovators and inventors and readily applied the available technology to their work. As a writer in *The Shaker* magazine points out, "'Shakers,' or 'Believers,' enjoy the products of nature, with which they are amply supplied and use all the comforts and conveniences which the fruits of their industry permit."

A watering "pot," or can, is an indispensable item. A perforated rose at the spout is perfect for drenching delicate seedlings.

The tools and implements listed in *The Gardener's Manual* will be familiar to all present-day gardeners and include such ubiquitous items as a rake, hoe, fork, spade, watering can, trowel, and so on. Larger items such as a plow and harrow were also suggested for those with large areas to prepare for cultivation.

Tools are most effective when used for their appropriate purpose. Such detailed information is given on the subject of hoeing that it is almost elevated to an art form, which we are told should be performed "with punctuality and faithfulness." The "three manners" of hoeing are flat hoeing, digging, and hilling.

Look After Your Soil and Your Soil Will Look After You

NURTURING YOUR DIRT

"Our lives are, for the most part, made up of little TRANSACTIONS, *and it is the true work of a benevolent heart to minister gladly to the little* WANTS *and* ACCOMMODATIONS *of every day."*

RESPECT AND VENERATION
DUE FROM YOUTH TO AGE, 1870

NEVER DOES THE MINISTERING to the "little wants and accommodations of every day" bear more reward in the garden than in the careful preparation and cultivation of the soil. Look after your soil, and your soil will look after you. *The Gardener's Manual* provides exact recipes for soil enrichment and explains that "experience has proved that the crop will be improved by good cultivation, both in quantity and quality, more than in proportion to the additional expense incurred, till perfection is attained, where, of course, improvement must stop."

The prescribed Shaker route to attaining perfection is often a prosaic one and this is especially true when tackling the often arduous job of soil improvement! However hard or unpleasant the work may be, it should always be remembered: "That which has itself the highest use, possesses the greatest beauty."

The Shakers often used the addition of tan bark or sawdust to improve the condition of heavy soils.

Soil improvement

After clearing your plot of turf, the ground will benefit considerably from a period of growing a vigorous crop, such as potatoes. This will break up the soil, which will then be ready to be "plentifully manured."

The finest manure compost should include mineral substances such as ashes, lime, sand, clay, or salt. Weeds, straw, leaves, along with the roots and stems of plants, all contribute vegetable matter. Spread in the fall and by spring the ground will be "ready for action."

To Every Thing There is a Season

SOWING AND PLANTING

"...a time to PLANT, *and a time to* PLUCK *up that which is planted."*

ECCLESIASTES, CHAPTER 3

THE SOWING OF SEED is a crucial process and one that often intimidates the first-time gardener, but the Shaker manual gives very specific and detailed advice on this subject. Indeed Mother Ann's entreaty to "Arm yourself with meekness and patience" seems particularly appropriate to the practice of sowing seeds successfully. Of prime importance is the conditioning of the soil; ideally this should be completed in the fall in preparation for the following spring. The ground must then be leveled and raked finely. However, in areas where rampant crops such as beans or squashes are to grow, "you need not be so particular."

VITAL SUNSHINE

Fall sowing is advisable for a few crops, but most seeds are sown from midspring onward; little is gained by sowing too early. Even if you sow later than the recommended time, most seedlings will catch up in the warmer, longer days of early summer. Today many gardeners possess a greenhouse and prefer to start seeds off in this controlled and protected environment. Modern experimental trials favor sowing seed dry rather than soaking beforehand. The Shakers would sometimes soak seed in a very dry season, "but generally, if sown in proper season, all good seeds will germinate quite as well without soaking, and to the seeds of the cabbage kind, it is a positive injury."

If sown directly into the ground, most seeds will need to be thinned to the desired distance apart once they are of a size that can be easily handled. These thinnings can be transplanted to spare ground, but they often object, curl up, and die. Thinnings of leaves such as lettuce are delicious and can be eaten in salads. Once acclimatized to outdoor conditions, seeds raised in pots in the greenhouse transplant more successfully since their root system suffers less disturbance. All must be watered until well established.

A TENDING HAND

Shaker gardeners observed and noted the behavior of their plants, and what they learned in this way often went against the received wisdom. Their *Manual* notes: "A prevalent, but erroneous opinion concerning transplanting is, that it should be done just before a shower, in order to succeed well; but experience has shown that a day or two after, when the ground has become dry enough to work again, in the evening, is a preferable time, and perhaps, with the exception of cloudy weather, is the best that can be selected."

A Good Gardener always Heeds His Surroundings

CULTIVATION

"BELIEVERS *may not spend their time cultivating* FRUITS *and* PLANTS, *not adapted to the climate in which they live.*"

THE MILLENNIAL LAWS

THE GARDENER'S MANUAL provides advice on the main skills needed for the successful cultivation of plants: hoeing, weeding ("should be early performed and continued with persevering faithfulness"), thinning (which should be "seasonably and faithfully performed"), plowing, watering ("to plants in open ground, that have good roots, watering in the customary way, with a hand watering pot, is of but little use"), and bleaching (blanching). Careful cultivation—the vigilant tending particularly of young and tender plants—is an essential watchword in the Shaker garden. Above all, a plant should always suit its position.

Examples survive in the Shaker archives of highly detailed garden records kept by many Shaker gardeners and growers. These show how they meticulously and faithfully observed and recorded seasonal and annual occurrences such as rainfall, temperature, seed and plant performance, and so on. They duly learned from these experiences. The Shakers strongly believed that one should garden (and indeed live) in harmony with one's surroundings; one should never go against nature. The Shaker Millennial Law quoted is most explicit on this point.

The sowing and planting times given are those that are suitable for the region of Albany in New York State, where the *Manual* was produced. However, it does acknowledge that the differing climatic conditions across the country as a whole can mean that variations of anything between 30 to 60 days may be needed in certain areas. Therefore, "it becomes necessary for the gardener to notice the climate, season, situation of the soil, etc. to apply these directions to profit."

A Shaker garden always appears to be in sympathy with its surroundings.

Be Thoughtful and Regular

HOT-BEDS

"EQUALITY *in labour, all working for each, and each* FOR ALL."

MOTHER ANN LEE

A HOT-BED is a framed construction, 4 feet (1.2 meters) wide and of indeterminate length, attached to the south side of a wall. It is filled with a mixture of fresh horse dung, straw, and soil, then covered and left for a week to "cook." Movable glass lids are attached to the top, much like a modern cold frame, and bell glasses or cloches are also used over selective crops. Seeds can be sown directly into this cozy and snug environment, then hardened off and planted out much earlier than if sown in the traditional manner. "Such vegetables as are wanted for early use, or such as require the whole season to bring them to maturity, may be brought forward nearly a month earlier, by being sown early in a hot-bed, and transplanted in the open ground..."

The system is the same as that known as "French Gardening," used by French market gardeners since the seventeenth century. It gained popularity in England during the late nineteenth century.

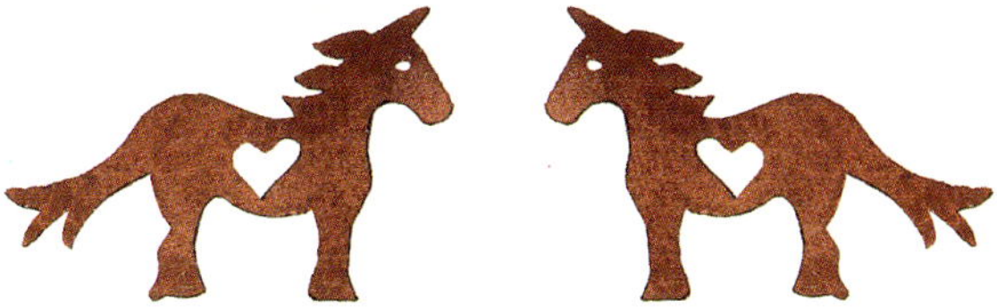

It is a system that requires constant attention to heat, ventilation, and moisture levels. Among the "Requisites for a French Garden," published in an English manual for commercial growers in 1913, the following were cited: "the personal qualities of cultural skill and dexterity, intelligence, and business ability and application."

For the hot-bed system of cultivation to succeed, a fresh and plentiful supply of horse manure is needed, not easy in these car-dominated days!

These exacting qualities demanded of the gardener are celebrated in the Shaker manual: "Many regard hot-beds as more expensive than profitable: but this is an error, they are not expensive property; it is true their management is quite particular, and requires you to be thoughtful and regular; but this is only promoting a good habit, and if you were inclined to forgetfulness, would almost justify keeping one expressly for that purpose." The passage somewhat stridently continues "...in any garden, worthy of the name, the benefits are double the expense." It infers that the successful keeping of a hot-bed is about much more than achieving a few early vegetable crops, and philosophically conforms to one of the Shakers' cardinal virtues: "Prudence and economy, temperance and frugality, without parsimony."

A Preventative is Ever Preferable to a Cure

PEST CONTROL

"Nature's great law is PROGRESS, *carrying up and* SUBLIMATING *each lower grade of being to subserve the grade above."*

THE SHAKERS' ANSWER TO A LETTER FROM AN INQUIRER, R.W. PELHAM, 1868

WHEN CONSIDERING the problem of dealing with garden pests in an environmentally responsible way, the Shaker philosophy of living in harmony with nature has particular resonance for the modern-day gardener. Unfortunately, it is not always easy to adhere to the third cardinal virtue of Shakerism—"Humanity and kindness to both friend and foe"—when confronted with garden enemies! Therefore, the recommendation made in *The Gardener's Manual* for "a preventative, which is ever preferable to a cure" is one with which few gardeners would ever disagree. Yet, even the most vigilant of gardeners can find their crops fall prey to "the ravages of insects." However, Shaker thrift and circumspection can do much to ameliorate even the worst of disasters, and a range of simple and inexpensive solutions was offered.

Organic pest deterrents from the Shaker archive

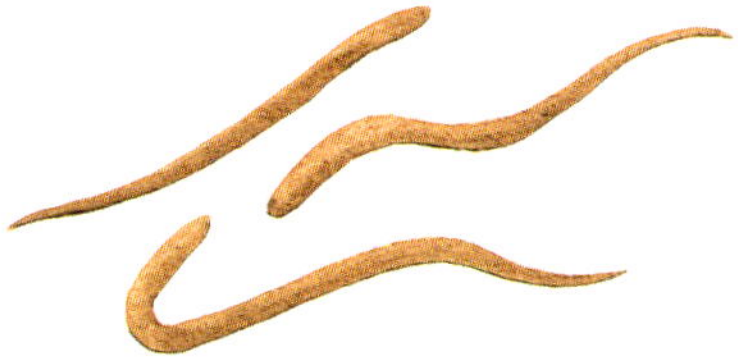

Root worms A solution of salt water was often poured over offenders. A scattering of coarse salt or wood ashes around the roots of plants was also widely used as a deterrent.

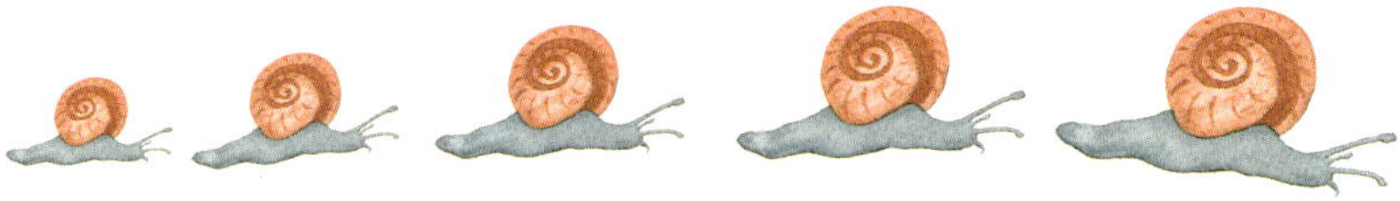

Slugs and snails These were often covered with ashes, and particularly valued plants were surrounded with sand or grit, which acted as a "modesty border," since both slugs and snails find this difficult and unpleasant to cross.

Turnip flies or garden fleas Young and tender plants of melons, squashes, cucumbers, cabbages, and turnips all benefit from a covering of fine shavings or sawdust.

Yellow bugs A mixture of rye-flour, ashes, and plaster was sprinkled over plants, also water soaked with cow dung.

RAISE STRONG SEEDLINGS

Judicious good housekeeping is as essential in the garden as in the home. The liberal sowing of seed should ensure a ready supply of stock plants to replace any that have fallen to the likes of the cut-worm, which, we are told, "commits its depredations in the night." Oversowing of seed is never profligate: plants can be given to gardening friends and neighbors.

The weakest plants are always the first to be attacked. Therefore, the gardener must do his or her utmost to raise strong, vigorous, healthy plants because "those who have the most good thrifty plants will suffer least." Vigilance, attendance to detail, and hard work are the gardener's best defense, and a prolific crop their reward. As another cardinal virtue advises, be "industrious, yet not slavish; that all may be busy, peaceable, and happy."

Modern applications for old wisdom

Today's vegetable gardener will find much appeal in the Shaker approach to pest problems. It is far better for the soil, and the food we grow, to reach for safe, inexpensive, and readily available solutions, rather than for toxic chemicals. The domestic kitchen is a convenient source of useful insect deterrents, such as salt. Crushed eggshells can be used as a substitute for the grit and sand advised by the Shakers to deter slugs and snails, and is biodegradable to boot!

HEALTHY PLANTS CAN BEST RESIST PEST ATTACK.

Perfect Partners

COMPANION PLANTING

"MANKIND *are yet ignorant of* NATURE'S LAWS. *They do not comprehend her system of checks and balances, her grand scheme of* SUPPLY *and* DEMAND."

THE SHAKERS' ANSWER TO A LETTER FROM AN INQUIRER, R.W. PELHAM, 1868

SURVIVING RECORDS show that Shaker gardeners would endlessly experiment and innovate in an effort to produce healthier, tastier, and more abundant harvests. The following observation appeared in *The Shaker Manifesto* of 1878: "We tested the plan of strewing tomato vines under plum trees, as a preventative of the curculio; and on a tree that we have invariably lost all, or nearly every plum, we had a nice quantity of the most beautiful fruit. We shall practice this simple provision."

AN UNUSUAL DETERRENT

In much the same spirit, the modern-day organic gardener will patiently test and try new ways to sustain as natural as possible a balance in their gardens, without reaching for harmful chemicals. The long-established practice of companion planting is one of the most attractive and pleasing ways (both ecologically and aesthetically) to achieve this in the domestic vegetable garden. The notion of companion planting dates back to medieval times, when there was a belief in what was referred to as "sympathetic majic": certain plants, when grown together, were thought to be mutually beneficial. This advantage could manifest itself either as a perceived improvement in taste or as having a seemingly deterrent effect on predators.

THE EVER-HUNGRY SNAIL

Whatever the veracity of these notions, what is undoubtedly true is the general improvement to the health and vigor of all plant life when it is grown within as diverse a system as possible. For example, a large area of land covered by a single species of plant, such as a field of corn, acts as a neon beacon to the hordes of insects that are especially partial to that particular plant (and usually necessitates a heavy spraying of chemicals).

However, if a mixture of plants is grown alongside each other, such as herbs, flowers, and vegetables, a more diverse and balanced insect and bird life is attracted and supported. And the chances are, that among this buzzing and teeming insect community, the ratio of "useful" predators to "harmful" or destructive insects will be the greater. Therefore, a wholesale successful attack on any one type of plant by a particular predator is far less likely. A perfect example of natural law, of Nature's "checks and balances, her grand scheme of supply and demand."

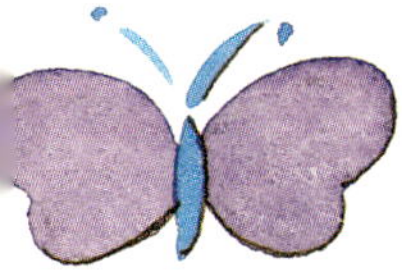

ENCOURAGE RDS, BUTTERFLIES, AND BEES.

SOME EXAMPLES OF GOOD COMPANIONS

The gardener's friends versus the gardener's foes

To attract beneficial predators (the ones that eat the "bad guys" such as aphids, slugs, and snails) into your garden, you will need to some extent to relax the Shaker-style urge to create "order" in favor of "usefulness and beauty." A certain level of tolerance of such profligate (and sometimes untidy) self-seeders as poppies, evening primroses, and forget-me-nots will be needed. Hoverflies are probably one of the gardener's greatest allies because they happily feast on the larvae of the enemy aphid.

THE BENEFICIAL HOVERFLY

The health and taste of tomatoes is much enhanced when grown together with the flower, French marigold and the herb, basil. Tomatoes, basil, and olive oil also make a classic salad.

BASIL

Good companions

The French marigold is one of the most useful companion plants. It attracts hoverflies and is said to be beneficial to tomatoes (it improves their flavor if grown close by) along with potatoes and cabbages.

Plant chives among your carrots to deter the carrot fly, which is confused by the strong smell of the herb.

Garlic is said to have a similar effect in deterring aphids on roses if planted nearby.

The herbs dill and fennel both attract hoverflies and parasitic wasps. They also have culinary uses in the kitchen.

It is widely believed that the following plants, when grown together, enjoy improved flavor: carrots and onions, corn and potatoes, chervil and radishes, borage and strawberries. The bright blue and red of the latter would certainly provide a stunning visual feast, if nothing more!

A Simple Provision

CROP ROTATION

"SHAKERISM *combines science, religion, and inspiration. It is a* PRACTICAL RELIGION."

ELDER FREDERICK EVANS

WE KNOW THAT THE SHAKERS' approach to gardening was largely based on the close empirical observation of growing conditions and how these could be exploited to achieve the best possible results. It is therefore somewhat surprising that *The Gardener's Manual* does not advise on the established practice of crop rotation. Only a passing mention is made to the fact that, following potatoes, either beets, carrots, parsnips, or rutabaga (turnip) should be grown in the field to provide animal fodder.

The main reason to practice crop rotation is the all-important health of the soil. If a single crop is grown in the same place year after year, the soil will become depleted of the particular nutrients and trace elements that the plant needs. Rotation of crops helps "rest" the soil because many plants are far less demanding of the earth's goodness than others. Indeed, some plants, such as peas and beans, actually enrich the soil they grow in with nitrogen. Diseases

BEANS ENRICH, RATHER THAN DEPLETE, THE SOIL.

are also far less likely to be harbored in the soil if crops are moved regularly. That said, the spores of some diseases, such as clubroot, can be very long-lived.

As with so much in the garden, crop rotation is the ideal, but is not always achievable, especially on a small plot. Above all, the individual needs and requirements of the plant should always be paramount. The gardener must be prepared to be flexible and not plant a sun-loving plant in a damp, shady corner simply to adhere to a rotation plan! A disappointing harvest surely will follow. Also, the culinary likes and dislikes of the gardener and his or her family naturally should be taken into consideration. Do not grow beet if no one likes it; instead devote a small patch of your root bed to something more unusual, such as Jerusalem artichokes.

It is common to implement either a three-, four-, or five-year crop rotation. However, most kitchen gardeners with small plots find the three-year plan perfectly adequate. Plan your rotation around the three main groups of vegetables. Legumes: peas, beans, celery, celery root, zucchini, squashes, tomatoes, bell peppers, onions, leeks, lettuce, spinach, and corn. These beds should be deeply dug with manure or compost. Brassicas: brussels sprouts, cabbages, cauliflowers, broccoli, kohlrabi, rutabaga, turnips, radishes, sea kale, and Asian leaves such

SCARECROWS: ATTRACTIVE AND PRACTICAL

The plan on the right provides an easy reference guide to starting a simple three-year rotation plan. The green areas represent legumes, the yellow areas brassicas, and the brown areas roots. In a longer rotation cycle, an undemanding vegetable such as lettuce can often be fitted in with other groups for convenience, although it is best not grown alongside brassicas.

as bok choy. The brassicas should follow the legumes and the beds then will need no added nutrients prior to planting. The third group is the roots: potatoes, parsnips, carrots, beets, Belgian endive, Jerusalem artichokes, salsify, and Swiss chard. If your rotation is to be over a longer period than three years, the above groups of vegetables can be further refined. Some crops, notably asparagus and rhubarb, will grow only in an established bed and can not be moved from year to year. Therefore, it is important to start these beds in the most advantageous position from the beginning.

The Pure and Genuine

SEED VARIETIES AND CULTIVATION TIPS

"...a claim, as strong perhaps, as any that may be urged for the IMPROVEMENT *of the* KITCHEN GARDEN, *is its usefulness."*

THE GARDENER'S MANUAL, 1843

A SUBSTANTIAL PORTION of *The Gardener's Manual* lists the varieties of seed and gives advice on the best ways to cultivate them. The *Manual* was sold through the Shakers' seed distributors and, obviously it aimed to promote their business. Varieties were selected with care, "with a view to obtain those that are most useful from the numerous varieties cultivated in the country ... we can therefore recommend them to be pure and genuine." The Shakers encouraged gardeners to grow only the best seed, both in type and quality, offering several varieties of most vegetables. Some are still available today from heirloom and heritage seed companies. With the *Manual* as your guide, you too can enjoy the rewards of growing "the most useful culinary vegetables."

THE REWARDS OF GROWING
"THE MOST USEFUL CULINARY VEGETABLES."

“A catalogue of garden seeds raised and put up by The United Society of Shakers”

The Gardener’s Manual provides the kitchen gardener with sound and simple advice for raising from seed the vegetables that are listed. The modern gardener may wish to substitute a heated propagator or greenhouse for the labor-intensive hot-bed, and this will be perfectly in tune with the Shaker spirit of utilizing “all the comforts and conveniences” of available technology. With the restrictions of space and time imposed on most of today’s gardeners, one is unlikely to be able to grow all the Shaker vegetables. However, I hope that the following notes will be helpful when choosing what to grow. The list runs in the same order as that in the *Manual* so that they can be read in conjunction.

THE APHID-EATING LADYBUG

Asparagus

With a short cropping season and incomparable taste, asparagus is still considered by many as a luxurious treat, for “it is a very delicious esculent vegetable” and never more so than when freshly cut from the garden. However, such delight comes only after patiently waiting, because an asparagus bed takes three to four years to become properly established and productive (although crowns that are two or three

years old can now be bought). Many crowns will be needed to provide a substantial meal, so this is really a crop to grow only if you have plenty of space. The Shakers grew a variety called Giant, which is probably close to our modern-day Giant Mammoth.

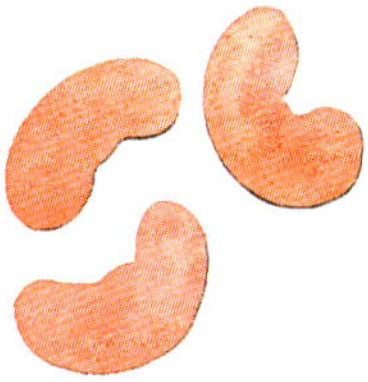

Kidney beans

Today these beans are enjoyed by many, particularly in Mexican dishes, such as Chili Con Carne, and in a range of salads. They are so widely available in dried and canned form that gardeners with limited space don't usually choose to grow them.

Runner (string) beans

On May 13th, 1831, the following diary entry was made by a Shaker named Phileman Stewart: "Have made my alleys with poles for beans and brush for peas, the result pleases my eye." The runner (string) bean is easy to grow, productive, and adds dramatic height to the summer vegetable garden. Known as "Running or Pole Beans" by the Shakers, they offered two varieties: Clapboard and Cranberry. In *The New England Farmer*, 1797, Samuel Deane wrote of the latter variety that it was "so named because it resembled that berry in shape and colour." Several varieties of bush beans were also offered.

Beet

The varieties listed include: Early Scarcity, the round-shaped Early Turnip, the unusually colored Yellow Sugar, Long Blood (which could grow up to 1 foot [30 cm] long), and Mangel Wurtzel. The latter was also known as Mammoth Long Red, with long roots and white flesh, and was often grown for cattle feed.

Cabbage

The variety Early York was popular and widely cultivated by nineteenth-century gardeners. It was featured in the 1881 D.M. Ferry seed catalog and was described as: "A very valuable early variety. Heads small, rather heart-shaped, firm and tender, of very dwarf growth." Other varieties supplied by the Shakers were Early Sugarloaf with a round, full head, Large Drummond, Green Savoy, and Red Dutch. This variety, later supplied by several other seed companies, was best used for pickling. Red cabbage is a versatile vegetable. It can be eaten raw, cooked, or pickled and is a useful accompaniment to many dishes.

Cauliflower

The only type listed is Early. However, because the *Manual* advises sowing cauliflower in the hot-bed in early spring in northern climates, it is unlikely that this is the same or even a similar variety known as Early London or Early Dutch, a nineteenth-century variety that was large, hardy, and suited to open field culture.

Carrot

The original wild carrot grew in a wide range of colors, including white, yellow, red, and purple, as well as the ubiquitous orange. The varieties Long Orange and Early Horn, offered by the Shakers, are both orange types that were developed by seventeenth-century Dutch breeders and popular with New World settlers. "Horn" refers to the Frisian Island town of Hoorn. They are still available today. The variety Altringham can also still be obtained. It is an early nineteenth-century English carrot from Altringham, near Chester. In its original form, the roots were long and slender, often measuring 20 inches (50 cm) or more. This made it difficult to lift whole, so commercial growers developed a thicker, shorter form. It is a high-quality seed and very productive.

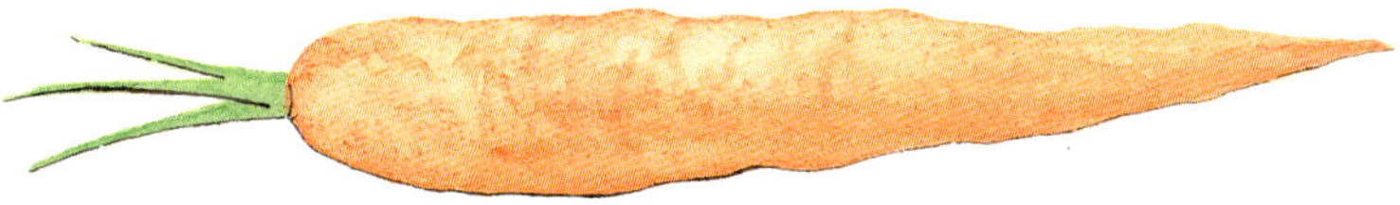

Celery

The Shaker variety is simply listed as White. It was obviously a prized crop, described as "an excellent salad vegetable." Much information is given about the cultivation of the plant and the somewhat involved process of blanching the plant prior to lifting, which is to be done before the earth is "locked up by frost."

Corn

Early Canada and Sweet, also known as Sugar, are the two named varieties. The latter, we are told, can "be preserved for winter use .... It then affords a wholesome and agreeable dish when cooked like bean porridge, or what is called *succotash*." Interestingly, a type of corn called Shaker's Early is listed in a commercial seed catalog of 1895.

Cucumber

Four types are listed: Early Frame, Early Cluster, Extra Long, and Long Green. Early Frame and Early Cluster are both American varieties suitable for pickling. The former is a very old variety described by Fearing Burr, Jr. in *The Field and Garden Vegetables of America*, 1863, as having "skin deep green ... flesh greenish-white, rather seedy but tender and of agreeable flavor." Certainly Early Cluster is still available and grows, as its name suggests, in bunches of two or three fruits. Long Green is probably a type that is also known as Long Green Improved. This is an enhanced variety of Long Green Turkey, introduced in 1842 and still available today.

Eggplant

It is not clear what color or shape of eggplant was grown by the Shakers. The color can range from white, pale or dark green, yellow, and deep dark red to the more usual purple. The fruit "if rightly prepared, is by many esteemed equal to eggs. Some are very fond of them when sliced and fried with ham."

To fully swell and ripen, eggplants need plenty of warmth and sun. Novice gardeners will often need to persevere! The Shakers started their seed in the hot-bed (the modern gardener will utilize the greenhouse) and the seeds were then planted out at the end of May. In *The Vegetable Garden*, 1901, Vilmorin-Andrieux wrote of the eggplant: "In England we have never seen this plant well grown even under glass. In the Eastern States of North America we were surprised at the fine health it attained in the fields, and the great size of the fruit—as large as well-grown melons."

Lettuce

Lettuce was obviously as popular a vegetable with the Shakers and their customers as with the modern-day kitchen gardener because several varieties are listed: Early Imperial, Early Curled, Early Dutch, Ice Cross, Cabbage-head, and Frankfort-head. Of the Frankfort lettuce Vilmorin-Andrieux wrote: "A handsome variety, resembling the Black-seeded All Year Round Cabbage Lettuce, but not so broad, and with a taller, egg-shaped head, of a peculiar gold shade." Unfortunately, I have been unable to find any of these varieties available today.

Melon

Of the three types that are listed—Large Water, Long Musk, and Nutmeg Musk—the Nutmeg is still widely grown. A standard variety—green-fleshed, juicy, and sweet—it grows well in colder climates. Melons specifically feature in one of the Shaker Millennial Laws: "Melons, and other choice or uncommon fruits, should be equally divided to the family... and no member should raise or gather them—to give to particular individuals to court favor or affection." This suggests that the melon was regarded as a highly prized treat.

Nasturtium

Nasturtiums were grown for their berries, which were pickled in vinegar and similar to capers, rather than for their flowers. Originally it was forbidden for members of the United Society to grow flowers purely for the appreciation of their beauty or scent; a flower had to be useful, not simply decorative. As time wore on, this rule was relaxed and eventually the Canterbury community sold ornamental flower seed, including hollyhocks, sweet peas, and zinnias, as well as seeds of medicinal herbs and vegetables. This 1847 Shaker song extols the beauty and simplicity of "lovely flowers":

Here Take This Lovely Flower

Here take this lovely flower
Thy Mother sent to thee
Cull'd from her lovely bower
Of true simplicity
Oh place it in thy bosom
And keep it pure and bright
For in such lovely flowers
The angels take delight.

Onion

The Shakers grew White Portugal, the American variety Yellow Dutch, and Large Red. Once successfully dried in the late fall sun, onions, like carrots and other root vegetables, provided a dependable winter staple.

Parsley

Seeds of two types were supplied: Curled and Double. Parsley, along with sage, marjoram, and thyme, is one of the few herbs the Shakers valued for its culinary properties. Most herbs were grown for medicinal use and supplied dried, as extracts, oils, or patent herbal remedies. Originally harvested from the wild, this herb was cultivated on a large scale from 1820 onward.

Parsnip

The only variety the *Manual* lists is Long White. It is an indispensable winter vegetable and a frost-tolerant crop. A quantity of parsnips was always harvested in November for winter use, while the rest remained in the ground until spring.

Peas

Several varieties are listed: Early Washington, the shelling pea Early Frame, the sugar or snow pea Tall Sugar, and Marrowfat. Of the American Marrowfat, D.M. Ferry wrote: "This variety is so well known that it is needless to speak of its good qualities."

The *Manual* gives the following advice for saving your precious pea seed: "If your seed peas contain bugs, we would recommend to scald them by putting them into a tub or pail, and pouring in boiling water enough to cover them, and stirring them briskly about a minute; then pour off the water and add a little cold water to them and sow them soon. This will destroy the bugs without injuring the peas."

Pepper

Three varieties were grown: Squash, Sweet, and Large Bell. Fearing Burr, Jr. commented that: “The Bell-pepper is early, sweet, and pleasant to taste, and very much less acrid or pungent than most of the other sorts.”

Pepper grass

This is a double variety of Curled Cress. The leaf has a mustard flavor and is used in salads. It was also used as a medicinal plant, North American Indians using the bruised fresh leaves to treat poison ivy rash and scurvy. It was also administered as a tea.

Radish

The radish was a popular vegetable of the time and five types were offered: Short Top Scarlet, Scarlet Trumpet, Long Salmon, Black

Winter, and Large Dutch. Long Salmon was listed by Vilmorin-Andrieux as Long Scarlet or “the Salmon-coloured radish” and described thus: “Root extremely long and slender… skin smooth, and a vinous red colour; flesh almost transparent, and slightly tinged with pink or lilac.” It is apparent from this enticing description that the Shakers not only provided "pure and genuine" seed, but also exciting and glamorous varieties. Black Winter is of a type that would be sown in May or June and harvested in November for winter keeping.

Rhubarb

Also known as "Pie Plant" and recognized for its value as an early season filling for desserts: "The stalks or stems of the leaves, cut up and prepared, are as good for pies as currants or goose berries, and six weeks earlier." The Shakers used the roots of rhubarb in their medicinal preparations, a tradition that goes back to ancient China.

A RHUBARB FORCER

The Shakers grew their rhubarb from seed, but commercially raised dormant "sets" are widely available today and should be planted midfall to early spring. *The Gardener's Manual* advises against letting the plant flower—"The seed stalks should not be suffered to grow"—although modern horticultural thinking is not so concerned with this. Enjoying the decorative blooms does not appear to have any detrimental effect on the fruiting powers of the plant. Rhubarb can be "forced" to produce longer stems that are ripe much earlier in the season. Cover the crown of the plant with straw in late winter and then cover with an upturned bucket to keep out the light. A more aesthetically pleasing terra-cotta rhubarb forcer can also be used.

A SELECTION OF SHAKER VARIETIES

Saffron

The Shakers used the flowers of the Saffron plant as a medicinal herb, rather than the pistils, which are used today for culinary flavoring and coloring. Their earlier, somewhat puritanical attitude toward the use of flowers would probably have blinded them to the notion of growing drifts of crocus in the garden simply for the joy of their beauty.

Sage

Sage was used by the Shakers for culinary, as well as medicinal, use. It is a plant much valued by the modern-day gardener because it easily fits into mixed planting schemes of shrubs and flowers, and the leaves can be harvested frequently without any visual detriment to the overall appearance of the plant. The purple-leaved variety acts as a striking foil to many flowers.

Salsify or vegetable oyster

Resembling a small carrot or parsnip, salsify is cultivated in very much the same way and, we are told, is "highly esteemed by those best acquainted with it." It is a vegetable that is worth growing because it is seldom available commercially. Vilmorin-Andrieux advised that: "The roots are sent to the table boiled, and the tenderest leaves form a very good salad."

Summer savory

The *Manual* advises using summer savory in the form of a tea because it "is a good remedy for the nervous head ache."

A USEFUL DIBBLE

Sea kale

How can you resist a vegetable that the *Manual* describes as "a capital article"? Originally a native of coastal areas, sea kale is little seen in stores, so should be grown by the gardener to provide a rare treat. Use a dibble to transplant the seedlings. The stems of sea kale are blanched before use to obtain tender, well-flavored shoots.

Spinach

Referred to as "Spinage" in the *Manual*, where the variety cited is Roundleaf. Easy to grow, versatile, and nutritious—everyone should find room for a few rows of spinach on their vegetable patch. Packed with iron, protein, vitamin A, and carotenoids, spinach is especially nutritious eaten raw.

Squash

Both summer and winter varieties of squash are listed: Sweet Potato, Summer Scallop, Winter Crookneck, and Summer Crookneck. The latter is an old variety that has an excellent flavor, described by D.M. Ferry as: "The richest and best sort for summer, very early and productive... covered with warty excrescences, the more the better!" Winter squash have excellent keeping qualities if they are thoroughly cured in the fall sunshine after harvesting, so they would have provided the nineteenth-century gardener with a valuable winter staple.

Popular with early American settlers, pumpkins and squash were often used as a substitute for apple and quince in old English recipes. Belonging to the same family as zucchinis, squash are hungry plants and thirsty feeders. They need plenty of space because they send out long trailing stems that bear several fruits each. Their large leaves successfully smother the growth of weeds.

LOVE APPLES

Tomato

Also referred to by the evocative name of Love Apple, this has only one variety listed in the *Manual*, and that is Large Red. This is still available as seed today and is a popular heirloom variety.

It is of a large, irregular shape that can weigh up to 12 ounces (350 grams). It is perhaps surprising to learn that a vegetable that is so widely enjoyed today was originally greeted with some skepticism. *The Gardener's Manual* claims of the tomato: "This is a very healthy vegetable, and a great favorite when we become accustomed to it, though generally not very palatable at first."

Growing your own tomatoes is one of the great pleasures of life for the vegetable gardener. The taste is invariably superior to the commercially produced item and the myriad seed varieties offer endless scope for experimentation. Why stick to growing the Shaker's Large Red when there is so much choice of shape, size, and even color of fruit? Contrary to the early belief that tomatoes were detrimental to health, blamed for anything from a chill to the stomach to overstimulation of the sexual appetite, extensive research claims that tomatoes are full of vitamin C and the antioxidant lycopene.

Turnip

Again a popular vegetable; varieties of both types were offered: those that resemble a flattened ball and those like a squat carrot, including Early Flat, Flat Field, and Long Tankard. "Ruta Bega" is listed with the turnip varieties; rutabaga is also sometimes known as the vegetable swede. Turnips were grown in the open field for cattle feed, as well as in the kitchen garden for culinary consumption. They were said to be "excellent for sheep."

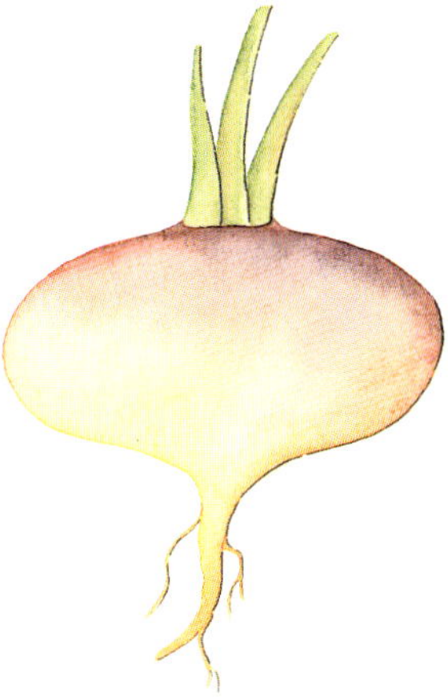

The Fewer Wants, the More Happiness

HARVESTING

"No idle drone within her hive,
will ever PROSPER, *ever thrive,*
then seeds of industry I'll SOW,
that I may REAP *where-ere I go."*

BUSY BEE, ANNA WHITE, 1860

THERE IS AN ART to harvesting fruit and vegetables at the optimum time to obtain maximum freshness, flavor, and nutritional value. Successful harvesting needs all the careful vigilance, detailed observation, and attention to detail that was so characteristic of the Shaker approach to life. Modern-day kitchen gardeners usually grow their own vegetables to ensure fresh and tasty food free from chemicals and preservatives, but the Shakers and their seed customers grew their food out of necessity. Without it, often they would have eaten little, or certainly less. Undoubtedly the best quality food is freshly picked and eaten quickly. However, previous generations had to make their crops provide sustenance and comfort

not only through the abundant summer and fall seasons, but also over the long winter months.

It was therefore crucial that the harvesting of the foodstuffs, which would become the staple diet of winter meals, was done correctly. For instance, cabbages were picked and prepared on dry days toward the end of fall. Beets and carrots would be harvested and stored before the first frosts. Advice for picking herbs and flowers of the "Sweet, Pot, and Medicinal" kind is much the same today as it was then. Herbs should always be picked early on a warm, dry day and carefully dried (the Shakers used racks or even kilns, but small quantities can be successfully dried by hanging upside in bunches in a well-ventilated room), and then kept in airtight containers or jars, preferably in the dark.

Some of the advice given in *The Gardener's Manual* is unlikely to appeal to modern-day tastes. Most gardeners prize the moment they can pick a fresh, fragrant, warm tomato straight from the vine and would never dream of heeding the following: "Tomatoes may be preserved fresh by covering them with sugar." Unripe green tomatoes were often "pickled, like the cucumber or pepper." Today the lucky gardener who does find him- or herself with a glut of tomatoes, whether red or green, is most likely to turn them into a delicious relish or chutney.

'Tis a Gift To Be Simple

PRESERVING, PICKLING, & COOKING

"When true SIMPLICITY *is gain'd,*
To bow and to bend
we shan't be ashamed,
To turn, turn will
be our DELIGHT,
'Til by turning, turning,
we come round right."

"'TIS A GIFT TO BE SIMPLE," SHAKER HYMN

AFTER THE SOWING, planting, feeding, watering, and harvesting of a vegetable, the final "turn" of the cycle is the eating. This is the moment, when through all the effort and care, "we come round right." Modesty is the note struck when offering up a range of mostly simple Shaker recipes, the writer noting "that they may prove beneficial to many, and a injury to none, is, our only intention and wish."

Nothing of God's bounty was wasted in the Shaker garden. What could not be eaten fresh was stored, preserved, or pickled. Directions are given in *The Gardener's Manual* for the preparation and winter cellar storage of beets, carrots, celery, onions, and turnips. Cabbages were frozen in a self-built outdoor "freezer," while all manner of foods were pickled, including nasturtium berries, bell peppers, beets, bean pods, tomatoes, and cucumbers.

Unlike most Shaker dishes, the recipe for pickling cucumbers is far from simple. It is extremely elaborate and lengthy and the trouble taken illustrates just how vital such preserved foods must have been to the nineteenth-century household. The *Manual* also gives directions for the simple cooking of such highly prized crops as asparagus and salsify. Today we might shy away from some of the Shaker recipes, as we all strive to reduce our intake of salt, cream, and melted butter! However, the recipe for rhubarb pie sounds quite delicious, seasoned as it is with lemon, cinnamon, and cloves. Try the recipe for tomato sauce—as different from commercially produced sauces or ketchup as can be imagined.

Tomato ketchup, or catsup

"Collect the fruit when fully ripe, before any frost appear, squeeze or bruise them well, and boil them slowly for half an hour, then strain them through a cloth, and put in salt, pepper, and spices to suit the taste, then boil again and take off the scum that rises, so as to leave

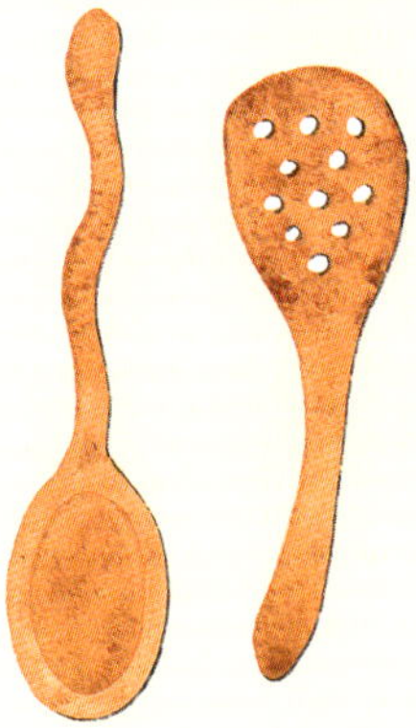

the liquor in its pure state—keep it boiling slowly until about one half of the juice is diminished, then let it cool and put it into clear glass bottles, corked tight and kept in a cool place for use. After standing awhile, should any sediment appear in the bottles, the liquor should be poured off into other bottles, and again corked tight."

Perfection attained

Just like the original Shaker *Gardener's Manual*, I hope this little book will help vegetable gardeners, whether old or new, cultivate a harmonious vegetable plot that not only produces a diverse variety of fresh and nutritious produce, but also steps lightly on the earth. Above all, let us remember that "a garden is necessary and useful, almost every body admits" and that one should therefore diligently dig, sow, water, and reap until "perfection is attained, where, of course, improvement must stop."

INDEX